The ADVENTURES of LIL' STEVIE

BOOK 2: FOOTBALL, FELINES, AND FAMILY

Steve Fitzhugh

TOUCH PUBLISHING

The Adventures of Lil' Stevie Book 2: Football, Felines, and Family
Copyright © 2014 by Steve Fitzhugh

ISBN: 978-1-942508-08-3
Library of Congress Control Number: 2015934226

All rights reserved. No portion of this book may be reproduced, stored in a retrieval system, or transmitted in any form or by any means—electronic, mechanical, photocopy, recording, or any other—without prior written consent from the publisher.

Author photo by Robert Shanklin

Printed in the United States of America

Published by Touch Publishing
Requests should be directed to:
P.O. Box 180303
Arlington, Texas 76096
www.TouchPublishingServices.com

To schedule Steve Fitzhugh to bring a high-energy, engaging, passionate message to your next event, contact him through his website: www.PowerMoves.org

Also through Touch Publishing by Steve Fitzhugh:
Pastor, We Need A Bigger Boat
The Adventures of Lil' Stevie Book 1: Canines, Campouts, and Cousins
Who Will Survive?
How I Lost 50 Pounds in 5 Seconds

This book is dedicated to the memory of my wonderful mother, Eva Mae Fitzhugh. She molded me, shaped me, and influenced me to be my best, have consideration for others, and enjoy life.

Through her difficulty and pain she never forgot how to celebrate each day. When I count my blessings, I count her twice. We'll meet again.

Contents

1.	A Day at the Pool	1
2.	Pooh, the Accidental Champion	9
3.	Football Frenzy	17
4.	An "A" for Effort	27
5.	A Tiger in the House	35
6.	Four Hours to Live	45
7.	When Momma Gets Cold	55
8.	Bustin' Suds	65
9.	Breaking the Rules	73
10.	Roslyn Sledding Championships	81

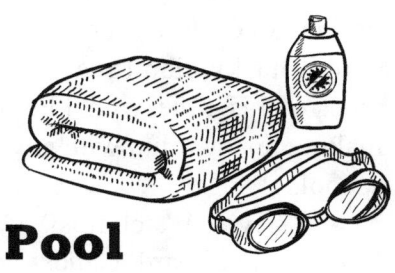

A Day at the Pool

One of the greatest delights of any summer day was a trip to The Pool. Lil' Stevie loved going to the pool. Stevie and his brother Chucky couldn't always get permission to go to the pool, but when they did, they were there.

"Chucky, keep an eye on Stevie and don't you dare let him get in the deep!" Stevie's mom instructed Chucky.

Stevie didn't know how to swim. Mom didn't have to worry about Stevie drifting into the deep end of the pool. Stevie was too afraid to do that. The only thing he had to worry about was a big kid dunking him under water or a bully throwing him into the deep for fun.

Walking to Perkins Pool was probably the longest regular walk Stevie's mom would allow him to take. For Stevie and his young legs, it was easily a five-mile walk. (The actual distance was only 1 mile, but when you are young, everything seems farther and bigger than they actually are.) It was pretty much a straight shot to the pool—down Roslyn Avenue, a left on Slosson, and a right on Noah to Diagonal Road. Some kids swam every day,

The Adventures of Lil' Stevie

some kids went to the lake to swim, but for Stevie a walk to Perkins Pool was a rare, privileged delight. Once inside the pool, Chucky didn't really keep his eye on Stevie. He spent most of his time with kids his age. Stevie found himself making his own fun with any classmates he recognized from school.

"Stevie! Watch this!" Chucky shouted from the ladder of the diving board. Chucky was awesome off the board and in the deep. Chucky climbed the ladder and proceeded to the end of the diving board. Then, like a professional diver, he sprang off the diving board high into the air and dove into the water head first with his two fists together breaking into the water.

"Wow!" Stevie mouthed to himself. Chucky swam to the side where Stevie was hanging on.

"Did you see that, Stevie?" Chucky asked proudly.

"Yep, I sure did!"

"Did you see the way I put my two fists together like Superman?" Chucky asked.

"Yeah, that was bad, man," Stevie responded with awe, trying to sound more cool than he was. Chucky returned to the deep for another round of diving. Stevie continued to splash and pretend like he was swimming. It seems like when you can't swim there is always someone there who wants to teach you, but never has the patience to watch you learn. Stevie was content splashing around in the shallow water or playing water tag with friends. Just when things were getting a little boring, Stevie saw someone that made the trip to the pool worth the walk. Crystal Starks.

Steve Fitzhugh

Although Crystal lived just across the street on Roslyn Avenue, and she and Stevie were classmates and friends, Stevie really liked her and always wanted to impress her. She had already impressed Stevie. She was pretty, very smart, fun, and could swim! Crystal didn't see Stevie making his way around the perimeter of the pool to where she was playing. She was preoccupied and Stevie noticed what had her attention. As he got closer, his heart sank... Teddy! Crystal was preoccupied with Teddy. ALL the girls liked Teddy. He could swim in the deep, he had perfect muscles on his perfect little body, and what Stevie found most impressive was his hair. Most of the black kids had small afros. When their hair got wet, it got thicker. It wasn't like that with Teddy—his hair was different. His hair was silky and curly even before it got wet. But when his hair got wet it didn't get thicker, it just kind of laid down. Stevie's hair, on the other hand, was tough before it got wet, and then afterward it got even tougher. The girls all thought Teddy was cute. Crystal had Teddy all to herself. It was like Stevie didn't even exist.

"Hi Crystal!" Stevie shouted out to Crystal.

"Hi Stevie," Crystal responded, not wanting to forfeit her capture of Teddy. It didn't seem like a real "hi," it was more like a courtesy "hi because you said hi to me" sort of thing. Crystal quickly resumed her playtime with Teddy.

Wow, it was like I wasn't even here, Stevie thought to himself. *Why don't I know how to swim? Why is my hair not like Teddy's? How come I don't have the courage to tell Crystal that I like her?* Stevie mused over these questions as he headed back to the shallow end to play with the other non-swimmers. The day started out so promising, but now Stevie was ready to go home. There were still two more hours left before the pool would close. Chucky was insistent on swimming for every moment that swimming on that hot summer day was available. Stevie motioned to Chucky.

"I'm going to go ahead and change. I am done," Stevie notified his big brother.

"OK, Stevie. Go ahead to the locker room and change. Don't go out of the pool entrance, just wait for me and when it's over we can leave together," Chucky instructed.

When Stevie began to change back into his shorts, he noticed that in his excitement to get into the water earlier in the day, he forgot to take off his underpants before he put on his swim trunks. Now his underwear were soaking wet. He got dressed without them, wrapping them up in his towel with his swim trunks. When Chucky finished swimming, he collected Stevie outside of the changing rooms.

A few of Chucky's friends joined him and Stevie for the "long" walk home. Several kids were headed in the same direction—even Crystal and Teddy. Walking with his big brother and his friends, Stevie tried to ignore Crystal and Teddy, but he kept peeking at them and listening. Crystal was all smiles. Stevie noticed another impressive trait of Teddy's. Teddy could squirt-spit. That's when, with just a little push of your tongue, you squirt spit between the gap in your front two teeth. It was soooo cool. If, like Stevie, you didn't have a gap between your front two teeth, then it wouldn't happen. Teddy had a medium-sized gap between his front teeth, perfect for squirt-spitting for distance. Stevie didn't remember Teddy living in his direction. Maybe he and Crystal were more than just friends and he was walking her home? Whatever the reason, Stevie was silently uncomfortable that the girl he liked, who was his friend, was walking with someone else.

Teddy's street happened to be not too far from the pool. Stevie's anticipated long, uncomfortable walk changed quickly when Teddy left. Crystal was walking only with her sisters now. Stevie saw his opportunity and decided to act.

"Courage!" Stevie whispered aloud. Stevie made his way over to the Stark girls; Crystal, Wendy, and Monica. Including Chucky and Steve, there were about 11 kids walking home from the pool together. There were too many to walk on the sidewalk, so they were spread across the street. Stevie finally caught up with Crystal.

"You have fun today, Crystal?" Stevie asked.

"It was fun Stevie, what about you?" Crystal responded.

"I always have fun swimming."

"But I thought you couldn't swim," Crystal stated.

"Well, I do more splashing and playing than swimming," Stevie confessed. Stevie was quickly running out of things to say. He wanted so badly to impress Crystal and get her mind off of the perfect boy, Teddy. Nothing came to mind. Stevie had no idea that one of his life's most embarrassing moments was only seconds away. There was an excitement of walking home with Crystal. Stevie wanted it to last as long as possible. Even in silence he was still content because he was spending time with Crystal. Then it happened. The unthinkable. The unimaginable. Walking next to Crystal, and trying to be a cool guy who could swing his towel, one end of the towel slipped out of Stevie's hand. Stevie looked up as his towel unrolled in the air. Almost in slow motion, above his head, Stevie saw his wet trunks and UNDERWEAR fly through the air. Plopping right down on the hot pavement, only two steps in front of Crystal, SMACK! went Stevie's underwear. It seemed like time and the motion of the universe froze when Crystal screamed in laughter.

"Stevie's *draws* dropped out the sky!"

"Draws" was how the kids pronounced "drawers," another word for underpants. EVERYBODY laughed. There was no way to ignore your own wet underwear, that you forgot to take off before you put on your swim trunks, especially when they are right in front of you. Stevie quickly scooped them up and rolled them back into his towel. Stevie laughed a fake laugh as if he wasn't embarrassed. Now the walk he wanted to last forever couldn't be over soon enough. It didn't seem to be a big deal to the bigger kids, but to Stevie and the Stark girls it was a riot.

Later that night, when Stevie was preparing for bed, he said his normal prayers, but this time he added something different. "Dear God, I wish I had hair like Teddy. Please God, when I wake up in the morning, let my hair be like Teddy's hair."

The next morning Stevie jumped out of bed, ran as fast as he could to the bathroom. Turning to the mirror with his eyes closed, he slowly opened his eyes, one at a time... nope. The same hair he went to bed with was the hair he got up with. God didn't answer his prayer. With such commotion Stevie had not noticed that his mom was watching the whole time.

"What are you doing, boy?" Mom asked.

Stevie told his mom about Teddy's hair and his prayer.

"No, no, no, son! You don't want to pray those kinds of prayers. God made you and everybody exactly the way you are. And God don't make no mistakes. He knows what kind of hair he gave you, what kind of nose you have, and ears, too. It's not good or bad, it's just different. Different is good. Most boys and girls your age gonna look completely different when they grow up anyway, child. Thank God for differences, that's what makes you special. If you spend all your time trying to act like and be like Teddy, you will only end up being a fake. Be the original you were born to be, son. The original is always more valuable than the counterfeit."

Stevie turned, looked back in the mirror and a big smile eased across his face.

"I am me... and I like me!" Stevie pronounced.

Stevie learned a powerful lesson through his trip to the pool. His mom taught him how important it is to just be yourself. Anyone can try to be like everyone else. The real winners learn how to be the best original they can be. Stevie learned that all you really have that's all yours for all your life is you. If you spend your time trying to be someone you are not, you will never be the one of a kind you were born to be.

Pooh, the Accidental Champion

Each day of summer vacation began with trying to figure out what adventure would be next. Lil' Stevie loved summer vacation. No school. No worries. Play, play, play all day. Since his family couldn't afford to travel during the summer, or do many of the things other families did during the summer, Stevie had to be very creative with his play options.

When he was young, Stevie would get his toys out and play at home. His toy car collection was his favorite. He had two types of cars. The bigger cars were plastic with rolling wheels that resembled real life cars. He would bring the broom outside and in the loose, unpaved gravel of his garage floor, he'd make streets with smooth strokes of the broom.

"Vroom vroom!" Stevie mimicked the sound of his favorite car. It was a red corvette. He'd pretend he was chasing down bad guys in the made up city streets of his garage. Although it was a lot of fun, he sure got dirty. When he got a little older, he had a Hot Wheels collection. Hot

The Adventures of Lil' Stevie

Wheels cars were made of metal. Some had doors that opened and closed or even a hood that open and displayed the engine. Hot Wheels came with orange pieces of track that could be connected together to make a race track. Chucky knew how to make the track circle around so when the cars went down the track they actually looped upside down. After a while of playing with his miniature cars, Stevie usually got bored. He wanted to be outside.

In the summer, the city scheduled what they called "recreation" at the different schools around town. At certain hours you could go to the nearest school that hosted recreation and get involved in organized activities. They had ping-pong (which Stevie didn't do very well), Caroms (which was like pool using wooden pieces instead of balls), and sometimes rollerskating. Schumacher Elementary School, Stevie's school, is where Stevie went to recreation. One summer afternoon, he was hanging out at recreation with his friend Lawrence. Lawrence was in Stevie's class at school and was one of Stevie's favorite hangout buddies. When there were a lot of kids at recreation it could be fun. But on a day like this one, when only a few students were there, it got old pretty quick.

"I'm bored Stevie, how long are you going to stay here?" Lawrence asked.

"I don't know. There's not much else to do," Stevie responded.

"You want to go bike riding?" Lawrence suggested.

"Man, it's too hot to be doing all that pedaling," Stevie complained.

"Let's go over to the Y and see what's going on over there," Lawrence said.

The two boys went to the YMCA, which was just next to the school. The Y had an indoor basketball court as well as other games. The big kids went there mostly to "run a few games" of basketball. Chucky was always there. Stevie and Lawrence walked in and saw it was just as empty as recreation was.

"You got any money for a pop?" Lawrence asked.

"Nope!" Stevie said in regret.

"I got a quarter. I'll buy one you can use the tab," Lawrence said to Stevie. The pop machine at the Y was pretty tricky. Chucky showed Stevie the trick. If you pull the tab off the pop can and bend it just right you could put it back in and the machine will think it was a quarter. Lawrence got his soda and gave the tab off his can to Stevie. Stevie bent the tab the way Chucky showed him and got his favorite Orange Crush. There was a sign on the pop machine announcing a pet dog competition that was to start in just 25 minutes.

"Lawrence, I think I'm going to get in this competition with my dog, Pooh."

"What can your dog do?" Lawrence asked.

"He can do all sorts of things," Stevie responded, even though he couldn't think of anything in particular. Lawrence, unimpressed, decided to head home. Stevie bolted out of the Y and down Lawton Street to Roslyn Avenue to fetch his dog.

"Why are you busting in here like that, boy? Slow

down!" Stevie's mom insisted.

"There's a dog show competition at the Y in a few minutes. It's free, so I'm going to enter Pooh," Stevie explained, still breathing heavy from his short run home. Stevie was so excited. His mom smiled and offered some last minute instructions.

"Make sure you put his leash on!" Mom exclaimed. Stevie grabbed Pooh, who had no idea what was going on. He was just happy Stevie was taking him along for another adventure. They rushed back up to the Y just in time to participate in the loosely-organized competition. To Stevie's surprise there were only two other competitors. In the field between the school and the Y, the staff person announced they were ready to start the competition.

"Since there are only three of you, each of you are guaranteed at least a ribbon. We have 1st place, 2nd Place, and 3rd place ribbons. Who would like to go first?"

"I will! I will!" said a young girl with a dog bigger than she was.

"What will your dog do for us today?" asked the staff person.

"My dog can roll over!" she said. The young girl shouted a command to her big dog. "Russell, roll over!"

Russell? Who would name their dog Russell? Stevie thought to himself. *I mean, there is nothing wrong with the name Russell, it just doesn't seem like a dog's name.*

As much as she shouted, the more the dog just stared at her like she was crazy. It was as if Russell never heard the words "roll over" before in his life. On top of that, it looked like Russell wanted a treat just for being a dog and sitting still. The girl couldn't have been more embarrassed.

"OK! Great job!" said the lady running the contest.

Great job? Stevie thought. *Did she see the same dog I saw? What part of doing nothing is a great job? She was just being nice.* Stevie guessed to himself.

"Who's next?" the lady asked.

"I'll go!" the other kid with a dog said. He was much younger than Stevie and the girl with Russell. His dog looked like Lassie. Stevie always watched the television show called *Lassie*. It was about a dog that saved people all the time.

"And what can your dog do?" the contest organizer said.

"My dog can jump," the boy said. He took off running as fast as his little legs could carry him, then all of the sudden, he jumped! The dog jumped, too. He didn't jump high or far, he just jumped along with the boy. It was cute, but it was not very impressive. Stevie thought for sure he and Pooh could beat both of these dogs. Just then, the little boy was running back in the opposite direction.

"Jump, Rex!" And then again he shouted, "Jump Rex!"

This is in the bag! Stevie thought. But what would he have Pooh do? *I should've brought a tennis ball. I could show them how Pooh can fetch!* he thought. Stevie drew a blank. He couldn't think of anything to make Pooh do.

The staff person looked at Stevie and said, "What's your dog's name?"

The Adventures of Lil' Stevie

"His full name is Poochie Rocket Fitzhugh. We just call him Pooh for short." Stevie reported.

"What can your dog do?" she asked Stevie. Stevie had NO idea what to say or do. The only thing that came to his mind was the word "run."

"My dog can run." It wasn't until the word actually came out of his mouth that Stevie heard how silly it sounded. *Run? All dogs run!* Stevie thought in amusement to himself. Now trapped by is own silly profession he had to show how his dog could run. Stevie and Pooh bolted down the field as if going to first base. They turned as fast as they could, like heading to second. They turned again like they were going to third base. And finally, as fast as they could, they turned again like heading home to score a run.

Chucky was just leaving the Y when he saw his dog Pooh and little brother Stevie zoom by. Chucky ran over to the competition just when the staff lady was about to announce the winner.

Pooh recognized Chucky as he showed up. Pooh ran to Chucky, who still had one bite of a Snickers candy bar in his right hand. Pooh jumped high into the air for the candy bar. Chucky moved his hand just in time. Pooh jumped again, but this time Chucky kept the chocolate barely out of Pooh's reach. This forced Pooh to stand up on his hind legs with his front paws drooping over like he was begging. Chucky then turned Pooh around like a ballerina by circling the chocolate around Pooh's head while he was still standing upright on his hind legs. It was REMARKABLE! Everybody clapped—even the two other competitors.

The lady from the Y made her announcement. "Well it's pretty clear who the most talented dog here is today!" Our winner of the blue ribbon and first place prize is POOCHIE ROCKET FITZHUGH!

Stevie was amazed. Pooh had plenty of tricks. Chucky came along at just the right time to get the right tricks to come out of Pooh.

Stevie didn't know it, but Pooh had built-in abilities that caused him to win the contest. Stevie tried, but could only get Pooh to show what all dogs could do... run. But when Chucky showed up, he was able to get Pooh to do some very special tricks. Don't limit yourself to doing only what everyone else can do. Sometimes, with the right push by your teachers or maybe your parents, you might discover built-in abilities to accomplish things that will surprise even you. Different people in your life will be there to help you learn and do different things. That's a good thing! Others can help you be just like Pooh, the accidental champion.

Football Frenzy

While Stevie was growing up in Akron, Ohio almost everyone cheered for the Cleveland Browns! Football was big and in the fall, everything was about football. Lil' Stevie couldn't remember life without football. His uncles were great football players. He'd often hear his mom talk about her brothers with such great pride. "Airborne and Seaborn!" she would say. Her brother Calvin was one of the best quarterbacks in the city, they called him "Airborne." Her brother Seaborn played on the same team and he was a big, strong running back. Seaborn was his real name. The dynamic-duo couldn't be stopped.

In Stevie's era, when it came to football it was always, "Raymond, Raymond, Raymond." His big brother Raymond was all the rage on the football field. Stevie was too small to understand exactly how to play the game. He did know that a touchdown was how you scored. He did know that when you scored you had to have an endzone dance to celebrate the score! That was the fun part for the kids when playing "free-for-all" at the local sandlot field. The field was just down the street for Stevie. It wasn't really a field, it was more like an open space between the Johnson's and the

The Adventures of Lil' Stevie

corner house. It was a lot where possibly a house could've been built, but wasn't. In free-for-all there were no teams. You'd just toss the ball up in the air and who ever came down with it would try to run to either "endzone" for a touchdown. It wasn't really that organized. Maybe the chaos made it more fun. Boys and girls played together. Raymond's football games were real—with coaches, referees, cheerleaders, and everything! Lil' Stevie and his family lived in West Akron. The team there was called the West Griffins. They were named after the neighborhood high school team: the Buchtel High School Griffins. They had Pee-Wees for the little kids called the Little Griffs and Bantams for bigger kids who weighed up to 140 pounds. Raymond played bantams.

"TOUCHDOWN, Ray Fitzhugh!" Stevie would hear the announcer call at Junnie's games. Everybody in the family called Raymond Junnie, which was short for Junior. His full name was Raymond Fitzhugh, Jr. He was named after their father.

"Ray Fitzhugh, the ball carrier, TOUCHDOWN!" Stevie was always so very proud of his big brother Raymond.

The little kids played in the summer, mostly before school started. This particular summer was extra special and extra exciting! Stevie's mom agreed to allow him to play pee-wee football for the West Pee-Wees. The big question among all of Stevie's friends was, "Who's going to play football this summer?"

Some played the year before with younger kids.

Stevie's mom wouldn't allow that. She thought Stevie was too small. But this year she gave the OK for Stevie to sign up.

"Mom, I need $25 to sign up for football!" Stevie said full of excitement to his mom. Money was always tight. His mom couldn't pay right away. She had to wait to put aside enough money that added up to $25. It came down to almost the last day before she finally had the money for Lil' Stevie to go sign up. There was a meeting down at Maple Valley Library, right next to Maple Valley Field, located near the corner of Hawkins Avenue and Copley Road. The coach was there taking money, signing kids up, and filling the parents in on the practice and game schedule. After the money was paid and the meeting was done, everyone went outside. The coach had most of the equipment packed into his car and began passing it out to those who had paid the fees. Stevie was so proud to pay his money and get his equipment. He tried on the helmet for a good fit. He didn't know exactly what a good fit was supposed to feel like.

"How's that feel on ya head?" Chucky asked.

"I don't know, I guess it feels OK," Stevie responded casually. Stevie was glad Chucky was there. Chucky was not only a big brother, sometimes he was like a dad, helping Stevie to do all the things that he had to get done.

"Snap the chinstrap. I'm going to tug on your face mask to see if this thing fits," Chucky instructed. Stevie adjusted the chinstrap so it would snap tight under his chin. Chucky gave the helmet a yank and a push and a pull. It jerked Stevie around a bit. It was kinda fun and made Stevie giggle. But the helmet stayed on. That was a good thing.

"Yep, it fits! I think you're ready," Chucky concluded.

"Alright guys bring it up!" demanded the coach, with a blow on his whistle. All the kids, Lil' Stevie's first football team, gathered around. "Our first practice is Monday at 5:00 sharp. I want you to come suited up and ready to go. You cannot practice if you have not had your physical yet. You can run all during practice but you will not be able to have any full pads hitting unless you've had your physical. Welcome to the West Pee-Wees! See you Monday."

Stevie had no idea what a physical was. "What's a physical, Chucky?" Stevie asked his brother.

"You gotta have a doctor check you out to make sure you're OK to play sports," Chucky explained.

"Does it costs?

"Yep!" Chucky confessed.

"Mom doesn't have the money to pay for a physical. If it takes her as long to get money to pay for a physical as long as it took her to get that $25 football fee, I might miss the first two weeks of the season. The season's not even that long," Stevie fumed, getting more anxious as he spoke.

"Ask Daddy! Just call him and tell him you need to see Dr. Wilacy for a physical. Me and Raymond always go to him for our physicals," Chucky suggested.

Stevie did just what Chucky said. He called their father and sure enough he was quick to offer the money to see Dr. Wilacy. Stevie's mom set up the appointment. Stevie was excited that he wouldn't miss any practice time because his physical would be complete before the first practice.

Stevie and his mom showed up for the physical. Stevie couldn't remember the last time he had been to the doctor. This was his first time ever with Dr. Wilacy. He was an older man with very short grey hair. It was so short that he was almost bald. He was chewing gum. Between the gum-chewing, and the way he barely opened his mouth when he spoke, his words came out like something between a grunt and a groan. Stevie couldn't understand a word he said.

"Geh ep uhn duh a'buh," Dr. Wilacy commanded.

"Hunh?" Stevie responded.

"Geh ep uhn duh ta'buh," Dr. Wilacy said louder, but no more clearly.

"What did you say?" Stevie asked leaning closer to be a better listen.

"GET-UP-ON-THE TA-BLE" the doc said slowly, as if Stevie was hard of hearing. Stevie wasn't hard at hearing. This man didn't open his mouth when he talked.

Stevie thought to himself, *I can't understand a word he's saying.*

"Nnake y'sherdof," the doctor continued.

"Hunh?" Stevie responded, feeling just as ridiculous as the first time the doctor spoke.

"Nnake y'sherdof bwoy," the doctor said louder.

"OK sir, I heard 'boy' at the end, but what was the first part?" Stevie asked sincerely.

"I SAID TAKE YOUR SHIRT OFF BOY!" the doctor said very slowy. Stevie took his shirt off. The doctor looked

The Adventures of Lil' Stevie

him over. He then put on his stethoscope.

"Bree," he ordered. That was easy. Stevie thought, *He wants me to breathe.* Stevie took a deep breath.

"Bree 'gin," doc said, still working over that gum in his mouth. Stevie took another deep breath.

"G'dnow uffa'ere n'pu y'shr'on," the doctor instructed. Stevie, thinking he knew what was next, hopped of the table and pulled his pants down. "WHAT YOU DOIN' SON?" the doctor asked slowly.

"Did you just say get down and take my pants off?" Stevie asked feeling a little foolish.

"No. I said get... down... off... of...there... and... put... your... shirt... on," the doctor said, with a short smile sneaking across his face. He couldn't hide his amusement of Lil' Stevie not understanding what he said.

Stevie passed the physical and showed up Monday for his first day of practice. The coach put Stevie at fullback. Stevie didn't know what a fullback or halfback was, but concluded that full had to be better than half so he was excited to be a fullback. Practice was fun. They ran a lot, did push-ups, sit-ups, jumping-jacks, stretching, and something Stevie never heard of, but grew quickly to dislike, called "six-inches." To do six-inches, you lay on your back with your legs straight and hands behind your head. At the coach's command you raise your feet only six inches off the ground until the coach says, "Drop'em, that's one!"

Sometimes the coach would make Stevie and the guys do twenty, holding their feet up for ten seconds each! That was tough. Lil' Stevie didn't know what that exercise was for, but it was the hardest part of practice. The coach had drawn plays on large cards that showed what each position was supposed to do on any given play. As a fullback, Stevie was mostly assigned to block, he just didn't know exactly how to be a blocker. He thought he could figure it out as he went along.

The center was the kid that hiked the ball to the quarterback. He also was in charge of setting the huddle after every play. "HUDDLE!" the center called, holding up his hand so every one could locate him. Since it was just practice the coach wasn't on the sideline, he was right in front of the huddle holding up play cards so every one could see. "I formation, 24 Power. Fitzhugh, you've got to hit the linebacker. Mosely, you hit the hole fast as you can! Run it!" the coach instructed.

The quarterback called the play. "I formation 24 power on one, I formation 24 power on one, ready BREAK!"

Stevie lined up where he was supposed to, the lead back in the I formation. The halfback Mosely was right behind him. The quarterback barked out the signals, "Down, set, 214, 214, HUT ONE!"

The ball was hiked. Stevie knew that the gaps between the linemen on the right side were all even, 2, 4, 6, and 8. The 24 power meant that the 2 back or halfback would get the ball and run through hole number 4. The fullback would lead the way. Stevie looked great. He ran through the hole clean as a whistle, untouched, and ran down field until he heard the whistle. Mosely got CREAMED by the linebacker.

"FITZHUGH!" the coach shouted. "I could have driven my car through that hole it was so big, EXCEPT for the linebacker. YOU'VE GOT TO HIT THE LINEBACKER!"

Embarrassing, Stevie thought. Everybody knew the coach drove a big Oldsmobile Electra 225. That was one big car, so the hole the coach was talking about had to be big... except for the linebacker. Everybody was watching. Teammates, friends, and even parents heard Stevie get yelled at. That was something new for Stevie and nothing he wanted to get used to. Even his mom didn't yell at him.

Hit the linebacker? What is a linebacker? Stevie thought to himself. The coach was pointing to Elbert Mclain, better known as Bubba. Bubba was Stevie's good friend, he didn't have any reason to hit him. Besides, he hadn't hit Stevie. They ran the same play a second time. Stevie did the exact same thing. He ran through the four hole, but hit no one, and kept running until he heard the whistle.

"FITZHUGH!"

"Uh-oh," Steve said aloud.

"We are going to run that play one more time. If you don't hit the linebacker, I will kick you right in the butt! They ran the play again. Stevie didn't really like to hit and so he didn't hit anybody, and Bubba smashed Mosely for the third time. Stevie was still running. The coach didn't blow the whistle. He let Lil' Stevie run all the way down to the baseball field before he stopped and ran back. The coach was silent as Stevie passed him and jogged back to the huddle. Without warning, a foot smacked Lil' Stevie square in the seat of his pants. The team and all the bystanders erupted in laughter. It didn't hurt on the outside, but it sure did hurt on the inside.

"I told you what I would do with my foot if you didn't hit the linebacker," Coach said. Stevie was too emotional to hear anything else Coach had to say. Back in the huddle Stevie saw his friends laughing on the sidelines. He saw Crystal Starks and her sister Wendy on their bikes, laughing along with everyone else. He kept his head down in the huddle so no one could see the tear that eased down his right cheek. Stevie was relieved that they moved on to a different play.

Stevie couldn't wait for practice to be over. He knew when he left the field that he'd never return. If this was what organized football was, he would rather play free-for-all. When he got home he told his mom that he really didn't want to play football.

"Baby, if you don't want to play you don't have to. I just wish you would have told me before we spent the money," Stevie's mom said.

Stevie never went back that year. Instead, he went down the street and played free-for-all with his friends. And one day, while down the street, he saw the coach's big Oldsmobile Electra 225 parked outside his home. Lil' Stevie was so embarrassed about quitting, he never even had the courage to return his uniform.

The Adventures of Lil' Stevie

If you are ever going to try something new, learn as much as you can before you start it. To learn, you must ask questions. Most of the time the question you are afraid to ask is the same question somebody else is thinking about asking, but is afraid to ask also. Asking questions is the smart way to grow. Stevie just didn't know the game, the plays, or the expectations. Whatever you do, do it because you want to do it, not because everyone else, even your brothers, do it. Stevie quit football that year thinking it wasn't for him. The truth was that it just wasn't his time. So he learned. He asked questions. The next year he really wanted to do it, he understood it, he played again and had a blast. He wouldn't let one disappointing experience stop him. He had the courage to give that crazy sport called football one more try. He was glad he did!

An "A" for Effort

One lesson Lil' Stevie's mom taught him early and often was that everybody is different. It's easy to get caught up trying to do things you shouldn't when you are trying to be somebody you are not.

"You don't ever have to change who you are just to fit in, baby. When you are OK just being who you are, you miss a lot of drama in your life, boy," his mom would say.

That helped Stevie so much. There were times that he didn't think he was good enough in sports like his brothers were. There were times that he thought he was too corny to fit with the "in" crowd. There were times that he was too quiet to talk to girls. That didn't worry him too much when he was young, but he certainly thought it would have to change when he became a teenager. His grandma also told him something that he would never forget. Grandma Angeline, his father's mom, always made Stevie feel special.

"It's the skin that'cha in that's most important," she'd report. That was her way of saying not to worry about what everyone does or gets to do. "Be the best Stevie you can be, honey. Let everybody else do what they do, and you do what you do!"

One thing that made Stevie very different was school. Most kids would love days off from school during holidays and summer vacations. Not so with Stevie. He loved everything about school. He loved class! He loved reading and science. He loved English, art class, and gym. His favorite was math. He absolutely loved math! It could be because his father studied math and something called physics and was very good at it. In the fourth grade, his teacher, Mrs. Wood, made a huge house out of construction paper. She put a window on the house for each student in the class. When a student showed that he or she could do all the multiplication tables through to twelve, they could turn their window from white to yellow. Stevie wanted to be the first to do this, but ended up second. Kim Sheppard and Stevie completed their multiplication tables the same day, except she beat him to the teacher to be quizzed first.

The principal made an announcement that interrupted class. "Attention students! The McDonald's Corporation, in an effort to encourage academic success, is launching a program for the first grading period only. When report cards are handed out, you can take your report card to McDonald's and receive cheeseburgers for "A" grades!

The class cheered. From the noise in the building you could tell everyone was excited about this announcement. This was too good to be true for Stevie. Since he was a good student, it was not a matter of *if* he'd get an "A" but *how many* "A" grades would he have?

Stevie sat next to his friend Terrence Scott. "Did you hear that, Tissue?" Stevie asked. (Tissue was a nickname for Terrence, after Scott Tissue brand toilet paper.)

"I sure did, Lump!" (Lump was a nickname Stevie picked up because of the shape and size of his head.)

"McDonald's!" Everyone loved Mickey D's! There was only one nearby. It wasn't close enough to walk to, it was definitely a car ride or a bike ride away. Stevie noticed a few students did not seem excited about the announcement, and he knew why. They were not "A" students. Stevie wasn't going to lose any sleep over that. He worked hard to do well in school and now the payoff was coming…McDonald's CHEESEBURGERS! Stevie couldn't even keep his mind on school. It was a good thing the announcement came at the end of the day because Stevie, like many of the students, was only thinking about the close of the grading period and all of free cheeseburgers they were going to be chowing down on!

Stevie rushed home to tell his mom the good news. He burst in the door and cornered his mom in kitchen while she was preparing dinner. "Mom! Guess what?"

"I don't know Stevie, what?" she said, pretending not to be interested.

"No Mom, you gotta guess!"

"I don't know… you found a million dollars?"

"No Mom, be serious!" Stevie scolded. You are NEVER gonna figure it out, so I'm just gonna tell you. McDonald's is going to be giving free cheeseburgers for A's

The Adventures of Lil' Stevie

on kids' report cards."

"Wow!" his mom said. "Stevie, you get A's all the time."

"I know, Mom! Isn't that great?" Stevie said, bubbling over with excitement.

"Yes, son, it's great. Speaking of school, do you have any homework tonight?"

"I've got to read," Stevie said. Every school day afternoon was the same. By the time Stevie came busting in the house, his mom already had dinner going. This day was one of his favorites. Mom's fried chicken. The aroma hit you before you even walked in the house. It was always hot, tasty, and crunchy. Stevie's mom was always home after school. She didn't go to work until everybody else got off of work. She worked the nightshift cleaning office buildings. Sometimes Stevie would eat right away and finish in time to walk his mom to the bus stop where she caught the bus to downtown Akron Orangerie Mall where she worked. Another reason Stevie would try to eat right away is because once his brothers were home from school they could eat ALL the food.

The week of the end of the grading period had arrived. Stevie and Terrence planned on how they were going to make the most of the cheeseburger heaven coming up on Friday. "I know for sure I have three A's," Tissue said. "What about you, Lump?"

"Put me down for four or five!"

"How you gonna eat all those cheeseburgers, Lump?"

"I don't know. I guess I better start making room

today," Stevie said. It was only Tuesday, but Stevie began cutting back on breakfast, lunch, and dinner over the next few days.

"Son, you didn't have much for dinner tonight," Stevie's mom noticed the night before report cards came.

"Mom, you didn't forget?" Stevie asked in disbelief.

"Forget? Forget about what?

"FORGET ABOUT WHAT?" Stevie mimicked. "This is McDonald's week. I'm not eating much so I can make room for my cheeseburgers tomorrow."

"Oooh Mom, can I have Stevie's second piece of pork chops?" Chucky spoke up.

"It's up to Stevie," she directed. Stevie was ssstttarrrrrvinggg! He wanted to fill up on his pork chops, but wanted plenty of room for cheeseburgers on Friday.

"Go ahead Chucky, you can have it," Stevie said, low and without energy. He tried his best to only think about getting three, four, or maybe even five juicy McDonald's cheeseburgers.

Friday had come. There were just a few details Stevie and Terrence needed to work out. The main one being: *HOW DO WE GET TO MCDONALD'S?* Terrence had a bike, but Stevie's bike had been stolen. Chucky had a bike, but it didn't have any brakes. As a last option, Stevie took Chucky's bike. The ride to McDonald's was all uphill. That would not be a brake problem. The ride back was all downhill. That would be a brake problem. Stevie left his house after school. All anyone could talk about that day was going to McDonald's after school. Stevie was so excited he

The Adventures of Lil' Stevie

almost forgot his report card. Stevie was very hungry, but his 5 A's were going to satisfy his hunger pain. He peddled quickly to Terrence's house, which was only a few streets over. It was work, peddling uphill. By the time Stevie got to Tissue's house, he was already drenched with sweat. Terrence came out and was ready to ride to McDonald's.

"Wait a minute. Let me catch my breath!" Stevie said to Terrence.

"What's up, Lump? I got three cheeseburgers waiting for me at McDonald's."

"I'll be ready in a minute," Stevie promised.

The two boys set off on their journey to Mickey D's. They rode and rode and rode and rode—all uphill.

"It can't be much farther," Terrence said, just about ready to give out from exhaustion. As soon he said that, a little dog with a big bark bolted after the boys. Stevie found it amazing how a little fear could turn weakness into strength. The boys easily out-distanced the dog, that in all truth gave up just as Tissue and Lump pulled away. They finally rolled into McDonald's. The place was packed. There must have been a lot of A's at Schumacher Elementary. Stevie saw Kim Sheppard (her mom gave her a ride). Stevie's mom didn't have a car. He never thought much about it, but today it would have helped. Stevie and Terrence were exhausted. Stevie was first in line. He unfolded his report card and handed it to the employee, who quickly looked it over and handed Stevie a cheeseburger.

"Next!" the employee shouted.

"Excuse me sir, but I've got five A's," Lil' Stevie

informed the worker.

"That's very good son, I'm sure your mom is proud!" he said. "Next person in line, please."

"Excuse me, don't I get more cheeseburgers?" Stevie pleaded, looking a little like he hadn't eaten ALL WEEK (which he hadn't).

"I'm sorry, son. The promotion is for one cheeseburger per report card with AT LEAST one A on it."

All Stevie could do was stand there stunned. His eyes were as big as saucers. His jaw dropped, his mouth was wide open. All he could do was think about all the food he gave to Chucky all week, making room for this day.

I rode that brakeless bike all the way here, and I've gotta ride it all the way back, past the dog, downhill, just as hungry as I was when I left, Stevie thought sadly.

Terrence was just as disappointed, except he ate well all week. Stevie had even given Terrence his lunch on Wednesday and Thursday. It took all of three bites for Stevie to finish off the lonely cheeseburger. At least Terrence shared a little of his orange soda with Stevie so he could wash down the last of the burger.

The boys began to laugh at themselves. "We've been dreaming about these cheeseburgers for three weeks!" Terrence said.

"Yeah, and we need to leave quick before Chucky eats my dinner tonight. I am starving," Stevie chimed in. The boys jumped on their bikes, zoomed past the dog, and headed back home. Since Stevie had no brakes, the only way he could stop was to stick one foot between the back tire and the bike frame and use his shoe as a brake. By the time he got home, he had worn a tire shaped burn almost all the way through his shoe. Luckily he was wearing the kind of tennis shoes whose bottoms were hard plastic and could last forever, even though the canvas sides wore out in a matter of weeks. They were affectionately called "K-mart specials."

Lil' Stevie's reward for his hard work in school did not satisfy him in the way he had planned. He thought that the benefit of exercising his mind would fill his stomach. What he failed to understand was that the benefit of a strong education is lifelong success. Temporary satisfaction is just that, temporary. A strong education is forever. That is the goal that is most important to be focused upon, not a silly cheeseburger that was gone in a matter of minutes.

A Tiger in the House!

Funny! Some people would say that all of the Fitzhughs were funny. Chucky was funny, Raymond was funny, Greta was funny, and even Lil' Stevie's mom could crack you up with laughter. It's what got Chucky into trouble during school at times. He was always making people laugh. Often Chucky could make his friends laugh and they'd get caught and punished while Chucky would get away with it! Stevie wasn't quite as funny. He always enjoyed those late night, nothing-to-do-times, when Chucky and Raymond were clowning so hard they'd have their big sister Greta doubled over in tears of laughter. Seeing his older siblings enjoying themselves with wholesome good clean fun was always a treat for Lil' Stevie. Even Lil' Stevie's dad had a funny bone. He had three or four of the same jokes he would say over and over again, even if he knew you weren't going to laugh. Sometimes Stevie would offer his father a courtesy laugh because he didn't want his dad's feelings to be hurt over corny jokes. For example, when it was time to go to the barbershop, Mr. Hodges, the

The Adventures of Lil' Stevie

barber, would always ask what kind of haircut his dad wanted for Stevie. His dad would always reply, "Just knock it down and bend it over." That was funny to Stevie maybe the first two times. But *every* time after that? Not really.

His dad also joked that Chucky was so skinny that he had to tie his legs into a knot just to make a knee. When he heard his dad kid Chucky like that it always made Stevie smile, but Chucky was not amused. The family humor came from Stevie's grandpa on his father's side. He was a part of a comedy team on a stage called vaudeville. Like the straight and funny man team in the old days of singer Dean Martin and comedian Jerry Lewis, Stevie's grandpa was the funny man of a two-man comedy team.

Raymond was the thick, muscular, athletic brother while Chucky was the lean, thin, swift athletic one. And when those two were together they did some crazy things. When Stevie's parents divorced, all the kids stayed with Mom. Since Mom worked evenings there was plenty of unsupervised play at night. Greta, the oldest sibling, was the built-in babysitter. One night Stevie heard Raymond and Chucky upstairs playing indoor-basketball. They would take a wire hanger and bend it into the shape of a circle. They would then open the bedroom door, stick the hook of the hanger between the top of the door and the frame, and hold it in place while they closed the door. The hoop was secure. If you opened the door, the hoop would fall. That meant if you were not in the room when the hoop was put in place, you couldn't come in. It was either in or out.

Since Lil' Stevie was too small to play anyway, he

normally chose to stay out. One night, Raymond and Chucky were going at it. They didn't have a real ball, but used a pair of white athletic socks rolled up and that was good enough. Even though it didn't bounce, they pretended it did. When the basketball game started, it sounded like a herd of cattle were upstairs. If mom were home, she'd put a stop to it. Greta didn't mind though. She stayed in her room and talked on the phone.

"Foul!" Raymond shouted.

"That wasn't a foul," Chucky insisted. Stevie could hear his brothers go back and forth even though he was all the way downstairs. After several minutes of arguing, the arguing stopped. Then silence. Then laughter.

"Hey Stevie!" Chucky called. "Come look at this." Stevie ran upstairs. The basketball game was over. The boys had moved on to something else, something totally ridiculous. Raymond had taken the plunger from next to the toilet in the bathroom and washed it. He then turned to Chucky, who had taken his shirt off. Chucky braced himself by standing with one leg forward and one leg back. Big, strong Raymond pressed the plunger against Chucky's flat stomach. He got the idea from seeing how the plunger stuck to the flat wall. The plunger was stuck to Chucky. Raymond maintained his grip on the handle. That's when the fun started.

Raymond bounced Chucky around by that plunger handle like he was an old raggedy doll. It looked just like a Looney Tunes cartoon. Raymond bounced him up and down, and back and forth, and left and right. Chucky was

The Adventures of Lil' Stevie

completely out of control. All three boys laughed hysterically at the sight. Each time Raymond pulled forward on Chucky, his plunger-bound stomach stuck out like he was nine months pregnant. This went on for quite a while. Breaks only came when the plunger lost it grip because of the sweat on Chucky's stomach. What a sight; two boys and a plunger. There was never a dull moment with these kids around.

Late one Saturday night, Stevie's mom announced that she was going to make it "Movie Night!" Every now and then she would come into a little extra money. And once the bills were paid, she was quick to arrange something family-oriented. The extra money could come from a bonus from one of the businesses she cleaned or a special gift from the family of one of the homes she cleaned. It didn't really matter where she got the money from for Lil' Stevie, because movie night meant PIZZA! Gino's Pizza on Copley Road had the most delicious supreme pizza. That's exactly what Stevie's mom ordered.

"Mom, are you getting Gino's tonight?"

"Now Stevie, you know I am. Why are you asking questions you already know the answer to?" Mom asked. "I got a little advance from Mr. and Mrs. Kliner for agreeing to clean their home the next two Saturdays in a row. I'll have some twos and fews to do something special tonight and maybe a big dinner tomorrow!"

Stevie's mom went out to pick up the pizza. When she returned, the smell of the pizza filled the whole house. Raymond and Chucky scurried downstairs to get their pieces. Greta made a pitcher of cherry Kool-Aid. Stevie loved Greta's Kool-Aid. She always made it too sweet for Mom, but it was just right for Stevie. The late night movie was about a ferocious tiger that terrorized the villagers of a small community near a jungle (or something like that). Greta had no interest in the movie. She retreated to her room for more endless phone conversations with her teenage friends. Raymond went to a friend's house. Stevie and Chucky joined their mom watching the tiger movie with the lights out. If Stevie was given a chance to pick the movie it probably would've been something different. But the Late Night Movie was the only offering that night for a decent movie. You were kind of stuck with whatever was on the three networks: ABC, NBC, or CBS. This tiger movie was kind of scary for Stevie. The tiger was huge with gigantic teeth. When he growled, you knew he was coming for you. He didn't just scare Stevie, he scared all the people in the village, too!

When the movie was finally over, Stevie sat on the couch next to his mom. He and Chucky had been laying on the floor close to the old black and white television to get the best view of the screen. It also helped to be close to the television just in case the picture went wacky and someone needed to adjust the antenna. Chucky went upstairs and Stevie didn't even notice. Still a little jumpy from watching that scary tiger, Stevie just wanted the safe and secure feeling he got when he was with his mom. He wanted to talk about anything that could get his mind off of that scary tiger.

"Mom, did I tell you what Mr. Albaugh said PTA

stood for?" Stevie asked. Mr. Albaugh was one of Stevie's favorite teachers because he said funny things.

"No son, you didn't. What did Mr. Albaugh say PTA stood for?"

"He said it stands for Push Teachers Around!" Stevie said, laughing. "Isn't that funny?"

"Now that's funny. Isn't he the teacher that got you calling the trash can file 13?" his mom remembered.

"Yep, that's him," Stevie responded. Mr. Albaugh treated the classroom trash can like a basketball basket. He would shoot his trash into "File 13" for "two points."

"I had my hands in that water all day. I can't believe they had so many clothes that I had to wash by hand," Stevie's mother complained. "My hands are so dry. Stevie can you do me a favor and run upstairs and get my Jergen's lotion off my dresser, baby? Your legs are younger than mine."

Stevie ran upstairs, which wasn't really running, it was more like jumping every other step. He got to the top of the stairs and made the U-turn to the left, past the bathroom to get to his mom's bedroom. Greta's room was right at the top of the stairs. A U-turn to the right and past Raymond's room would take you to the room Stevie and Chucky shared with bunk beds. The light in Stevie's mom's room was tricky. You could turn it on at the entrance unless it had been turned out over by the bed. If it was turned out over near the bed, then you had to go there to turn it on. The room was dark. All Stevie could think about at this time was that ferocious tiger.

Why did I watch that entire scary movie about that stupid tiger? Stevie thought to himself.

The dark room already had Stevie's eyes playing tricks on him. The dresser looked like bushes in the dark while the floor resembled the dirt floor of the tiger village.

"Oh God, please let this light come on when I flip the switch," Stevie whispered quietly, but seriously.

Lil' Stevie crossed his fingers and flipped the switch… no light. Stevie's heart began to beat so strongly he could feel it throbbing in his ears. He entered the dark room. He could vaguely see the white Jergen's lotion bottle just five steps in front of him on the dresser like his mom described. He slowly reached out to grab it. He carefully stretched out his arm… slowly… closer… slowly… closer. And just when his fingers barely touched the bottle, a tiger jumped out from beside the bed!

"GRRROOOOWWWL," it threatened in a deep guttural voice. Stevie ran like the wind! Fast as lightning out of Mom's room, past the bathroom, making the u-turn down the stairs, screaming at the top of his lungs.

"AHHHHH!" Stevie screamed. "A TIGERRRR!"

He was moving so fast his feet never had time to actually rest on a stair before moving to the next one. His mouth was so wide open his face disappeared. Fear had his eyes bigger than saucers and veins bulging from his neck and forehead.

"Mooooooom!" Stevie yelled. She had already jumped from her seat and was standing at the bottom of the stairs as Lil' Stevie rushed into her arms of safety, almost knocking her over.

OK, it wasn't really a tiger. It was Chucky. Chucky was at the top of the stairs when he heard the instructions for Stevie to get the lotion. Being the prankster he was, he quickly hid beside the bed. To Lil' Stevie this was for sure the tiger from the movie trying to eat him!

"Ch-Ch...Ch-Ch-Ch...Chucky scared me," Stevie blurted through sobs and gasps. Chucky was rolling on the floor, laughing uncontrollably.

"Stevie... haha... hehehe... wooo... here's the lotion," Chucky joked, still laughing so hard it hurt. "Oh, oh, oh Stevie... you killin' me man... a tiger... ahhh ha ha ha!" Chucky continued, completely amused at Stevie's flight.

"Chucky, why did you scare that boy like that? It's not funny! Go to your room until I come up there. You're gonna get a spanking," Mom warned from the bottom of the stairs. Stevie didn't want to see Chucky get a whipping. Even Stevie had already begun to laugh at himself. Stevie's mom marched upstairs. When Mom gave a spanking it was with the first thing she could put her hands on; a broom, a shoe, a stick. This time it was one of their orange Hot Wheels race car tracks. She made a lot of noise up there, but Stevie heard snickering too. He didn't think his mom was giving Chucky a real whipping.

There is an old saying that laughter is the best medicine. It may be fun, and even funny, to joke and play or even play a joke on someone as long as it's good-natured.

We've got to remember though that if we are not careful, someone may get hurt. People can get very seriously hurt when horseplay goes too far. It's never worth the laugh if there is a possibility someone may be injured physically or emotionally. There were no more late night scary movies for Stevie. The next time, a "Monster" just might show up!

Four Hours to Live

Lil' Stevie believed his mom was the coolest. She could do it all! She was an excellent cook. One Sunday, she was cooking dinner and amazement struck Lil' Stevie.

"Mom?" Stevie interrupted. "How do you do that?"

"Do what, son?" she replied.

"Do that. You know? You cook *all* this food at the same time. There's something on every spot on the stove cooking at the same time, and something in the oven too."

"Well it's got to be cooked, baby," Mom said.

"But how do you know what to do for each thing, and remember where you left off?" Stevie was really trying to understand how such a feat could be accomplished. "I could never do that. Something would definitely burn if I tried to do this."

"After you've been doing it for many years you just learn what to do, how much spice to add, how high to have the heat and so on. I've been doing this so long I can do it with my eyes closed," Stevie's mom said.

Stevie knew she would never cook with her eyes

closed, but he got her point. That was Mom. She had an answer for everything. Like the time Stevie was sad about his dad. We all get disappointed, but this time Stevie was really disappointed.

"Your dad loves you so much Stevie, he just loves you in his own way," Mom had said. Somehow that made sense to Stevie. His mom never had a bad word to say about anyone. She always looked on the good side of everything.

At the time of the divorce, Greta was 16, Raymond 15, Chucky was 11, and Stevie was 7 years old. This small family of five had to find a way to survive and all of the responsibility landed on Mom. If you ever met her, you would never have known she was under such pressure to provide for her family with only a high school education. She was so full of life, jokes, pranks, and pure fun.

One hot summer day the temperature in Akron, Ohio was extremely high. Their home at 1082 Roslyn Avenue had no air conditioning. The heat inside was unbearable. Even the heat outside was too much to play in. It was much cooler just to sit still and fan yourself until the sun went down.

"I can't take this today!" Stevie's mom said. "Come on Stevie, you wanna go for a ride?"

"Go for a ride?" Stevie asked. He knew that old beat up piece of a car his mom had gotten burned too much gas to go cruising just to cool off.

"I have an idea," Mom said. They jumped in the car. The gas needle as always was already on E for empty, so this must have been important. Stevie and his mom drove the short distance to K-mart on Wooster Avenue. Stevie's mom knew exactly what she wanted. She went to the swimming pool section.

"Mom, we don't have a pool. What do you need from over here?" Stevie asked.

"Today son, we will have a pool," she said. She went to the kiddie section and picked out a plastic pool. "Son, grab one of those blue ones."

"Mom! You can't be serious, Mom. These are for little babies!" Stevie cried. Stevie was almost bigger than the pool himself. But to his mom's insistence he grabbed the plastic pool and set it on top of the cart since it wouldn't fit all the way inside. When they got home, Stevie's mom changed into her bathing suit. She put the pool in the front yard, filled it with water and stepped in. She held the garden hose over her head like a shower and drenched herself.

"Ooh Stevie! This feels so good! It's so refreshing," she said.

"I guess I'll try it too," Stevie said. Stevie couldn't believe what he was seeing. At first he was a little embarrassed. Then he decided to take his socks and shoes off and step in the pool. But once his socks and shoes were off, his mom turned the hose on him and squirted him with a steady stream of cold water. Stevie tried to run, but couldn't get away in time. As hot as it was, the cool water felt great! He was laughing the whole time she squirted him. That was Mom. Someone might think that Mrs. Fitzhugh was a little weird. She wasn't weird to Stevie, she was just different. And she taught Stevie that different isn't bad, it's just different. Different is good!

Mom liked to barbeque. Some people only barbequed in the summer, when the weather was nice. Not Lil' Stevie's mom. She would barbeque out back on the patio in the snow or in the garage if it was raining. If she had a taste for some of her own barbeque, well then she was going to have barbeque. That was Mom!

Once, when Stevie was walking home from school, he saw his next-door neighbor Karen Tate, who was around Chucky's age, going into his home. Stevie thought that was odd.

As he walked up the driveway and got closer to the door, he heard classical music coming from inside. Once he was in the house, it finally made sense. Karen loved to see Stevie's mom dance. Although she had no formal training, sometimes Mom would put on classical music and twirl, spin, kick, and jump just like a ballerina on stage. Karen thought it was so beautiful. To Stevie, it was just Mom being Mom. Later that particular weekend, Stevie's mom said she felt like she had the flu. She was feeling pretty bad. It was so bad she had to go to the hospital.

She gathered all the kids together and said she was going to the emergency room to get checked out because she was feeling worse, not better.

"Greta, look after your brothers until I get back," she instructed. But that night, Mom didn't come back. Aunt Pearlie came over and told the kids that they were going to keep their mother at the hospital overnight to run some tests. Aunt Pearlie stayed with the children that night. The next day, their father came over. Stevie knew something wasn't right. It was rare to see his dad in their home. He informed the children that their mother had become very ill. She had an infection that Stevie not only never heard of, he couldn't even pronounce it. It was called Spinal Meningitis. *This was serious,* Stevie thought.

"Your mom is going to have to be in the hospital and on medicine for a while. You all are going to go to your grandmother's house for a few days. She's going to drive you to school," Stevie's dad informed, his tone presenting a great warning. "I want you kids to be on your best behavior. Mind your grandmother! I don't want my mother having a heart attack trying to handle you kids. I'm especially talking to you, Raymond and Chucky!"

Grandma's house wasn't that big, so Stevie didn't know exactly how this was going to work. He was soon to find out. Raymond, Stevie, and Chucky had to sleep in the same bed. Raymond was on one end, Chucky was on the other end, and Lil' Stevie was scrunched in the middle. Stevie was squeezed so tightly between his brothers, all he could do was lay there and not move.

Mom is going to have to get better quick, fast, and in a hurry because this is NOT going to work! Stevie thought to himself that first night. To top it off, Stevie had a bad cough that only got worse as the night continued. It was one of those coughs that sounded like a dog was barking. It kept Chucky and Raymond awake. Which made them very upset with Lil' Stevie.

"Grandma!" Chucky called. "Grandma! We can't sleep because Stevie keeps coughin'. He's barking like a dog. Is there ANYTHING you can do?" Chucky pleaded his case.

"Here Stevie, drink this water and be still, baby," Grandma said. "Chucky, you and Raymond try to go back to sleep when Stevie quiets down." Stevie did finally stop coughing long enough for all three boys to get some sleep. The next morning, Grandma took everybody to school and came back to pick them up. Stevie went to Schumacher on the west side of Akron. Chucky was at Simon Perkins Junior High. Raymond had to catch the big yellow school bus all the way to Walsh Jesuit High School in Cuyahoga Falls, Ohio. That was about twenty-five minutes away. While he was at school, all that Lil' Stevie could think about was his mom. He had so many questions. *Is she going to be OK? Why do they have to take so long just to run a few tests? When will this be over and we can go back home and do life normal again?*

After everyone was home from school that night, Stevie's father showed up around dinnertime. "After you kids eat I'm going to take you over to the hospital to see your mom," Lil' Stevie's father announced. Stevie didn't like the tone of his father's voice. It seemed like things were worse than he let on.

"How's Mom doing, Daddy?" Stevie jumped right in. "Is the medication working?" he asked anxiously.

"Your mom's fine. You'll get a chance to see her after dinner," Mr. Fitzhugh explained to his children. Stevie was very clever. He noticed that Dad didn't say they were going to "talk" to her but they were going to "see" her.

Does that mean that she can't talk? he wondered. For the first time none of the boys had much of an appetite. They liked Grandma's cooking, but they were much more interested in seeing their mom. When they arrived at the hospital, the doctor asked them to go into a private room so he could explain their mother's condition.

"Your mom has an infection called Spinal Meningitis. There is something like a protective coat for your spinal cord and your brain. This infection attacks that protective coat," the doctor said. Stevie could tell the doctor was talking kid-talk and not grown-up-talk in an attempt get the children to understand what was going on with their mom. "In cases like this, our best chance is to catch it early and give medicine to your mom to stop the infection while it's still in the spinal cord. If we do, chances of recovery are very good. It the infection reaches the brain... well... that's a different story."

Stevie could feel the lump in his throat and his eyes watering up before he asked a question.

"Where is the infection in my mom?" he asked hesitantly.

"I'm sorry son, that's why we brought you here tonight. The infection has already reached your mom's brain. In fact, it has almost completely covered her brain. It has been very aggressive and resistant to the antibiotics we've been giving her the last two days. The infection is tough, but your mom is, too. Eva is a fighter. At this point our best guess is she has about 4 hours to live," the doctor confessed.

All of the air escaped Lil' Stevie's lungs. Greta began to cry. Chucky and Raymond were silent. Stevie couldn't prevent the tears from beginning to pour down his cheeks. He was not at all prepared for this.

"You kids be strong for this last visit with your mom," their dad suggested. "If she sees you guys crying, it's only gonna make her more sad."

The nurse passed out protective masks for everyone to put on before going into the room. This was to insure that the infection would not spread to anyone else. For Stevie it helped to hide the tracks of his tears. They entered the room where Lil' Stevie's mom was staying. She was hooked up to machines and IVs and things Lil' Stevie had no idea what they were. They wanted to split up and go on both sides of the bed, but only had access to one side. Since they were all together, they found themselves holding on to each other as they approached their dying mother. It was one big group hug. She was asleep, most likely as a result of the pain medication. It wasn't much of a goodbye because there was no conversation; just sniffing, watery eyes, and silent prayers. The nurse came over to the bed and said she had to administer her medicine. She said the doctor would meet everyone in the next room and would like to speak to them before they left. The four children and their father stepped into the next room. Raymond was trying to be tough. That was the first time Lil' Stevie saw his big brother Raymond cry. The room was completely quiet. The doctor's entrance finally broke the silence.

"I need to inform you that because this infection has

infected the brain, if by some miracle she recovers, she will have lost at least one or more of her five senses; To touch, hear, see, smell, or taste," the doctor warned. Although the doctor was talking directly to Stevie's father, the kids could easily hear all that he said. The ride back to Grandma's was without event. Everyone was sad. All Lil' Stevie knew to do was to pray. Raymond didn't even go to bed that night. He and Greta stayed up all night worried about their mother.

Early the next morning, Greta screamed loud enough to wake everyone in Grandma's house. She came running down the stairs from the attic where she slept in the extra bed.

"I JUST GOT OFF THE PHONE WITH THE HOSPITAL!" she shouted. Stevie bounded over Chucky and out of the bed first. Chucky and Raymond stood behind Stevie in their pajamas.

"Well, Greta?" Raymond asked.

"Mom woke up this morning and asked for something to eat. The infection is completely GONE! NO SPINAL MENINGITIS!"

The kids shouted and jumped high as they could. Greta was crying tears of joy. "Mom has all of her senses," she continued. "It's a miracle. It's a miracle!"

In just two days Lil' Stevie's mom was home from the hospital. She lived a normal life, as if the sickness that was supposed to take her life or leave her handicapped never happened.

A wise man once said, "It's not over until it's over."

The Adventures of Lil' Stevie

We all face dark days in our lives, but that doesn't mean our lives have to be dark. That's why it's important to celebrate life and appreciate those who are close to you. We never know when our chance to love them will be over, that's why we must love them now. Think about the people you love. Take some time today to let them know.

When Momma Gets Cold

One of the most regular routines in the Fitzhugh house was the typical school day morning. Lil' Stevie's mom had it down to a science. Greta had to go to Buchtel High School, Raymond had to catch the bus to Walsh Jesuit High School, while Stevie went one block away to Schumacher. Chucky had just started Perkins Junior High. They all had to get up, wash up, eat, and be on their way on time. There was no being late for school in this house.

Bam! Bam! Bam! Bam! Bam!

Stevie's mom slammed the heel of her hand against the wall at the bottom of the stairs. "It's time to get up sleepy-heads!" Ms. Fitzhugh alerted her kids. "Junnie, Chucky, Stevie, Greta get up."

Everybody could take it from there and manage their mornings to get off to school just fine. Stevie's mom did the most each morning for him. He was her "Little Man," she'd always say. She fixed him breakfast, picked out his clothes, and when his face was dry she'd rub a little butter on her

The Adventures of Lil' Stevie

hands and wipe his face as if it was lotion. If she used too much, she'd wipe the extra butter on his shoes to give them a temporary shine. Although she only had a high school education she made sure all of her kids knew that the books come first. Stevie heard that so much from his mom, he was convinced that the most important thing in life was education. There was no skipping school unless you were so sick you were close to dead. There was never any reason to be tardy. Ms. Fitzhugh made sure her kids did their homework before watching television and when it was time for bed, the television went off! Everyone did well in school. School was the biggest part of Lil' Stevie's life.

One day when he was in kindergarten, he woke up late for school. He didn't remember hearing the pounding on the wall and somehow his brothers and sister got up anyway and were off to school. He bounded into his mother's bedroom. Stevie began to panic!

"Mom! Mom! Wake up! I'm late for school!" he told his mother, who was sound asleep. His mom had overdone it the day before. On occasion she would clean a home before she went to her regular full time job. But yesterday she was able to squeeze in THREE homes before going directly to her main job. The opportunity came and she really needed the money. But this morning she was completely exhausted. Lil' Stevie recognized this and decided to let his mom get her much-needed rest.

Stevie hurried into the bathroom to brush his teeth. He was going to prove to his mom he was a big boy. He dashed into his bedroom to pick out something to wear.

Mom always picks out my clothes. What will I wear? Will it match? Stevie thought to himself. Stevie didn't want to be laughed at during school. He remembered his sister telling him one day after he dressed himself that the "clothes didn't match." *Oh, I know what I'll wear! I will wear my Easter suit!* Stevie concluded. He was certain that would be OK, because it was certainly a match. For Easter that year Lil' Stevie got a brown pinstriped suit. It came with a brown shirt and a clip-on tie. All dressed up, he looked like a little gangster. Stevie went to his closest and pulled out his Easter outfit. Since it wasn't really Easter he decided to not wear the tie. He got dressed as fast as he could. He raced downstairs and decided to skip breakfast. His shoes were too dusty for his clean suit so he stopped by the refrigerator and put a little butter on his shoes to make them shine. He bolted out the door and hurried to school.

"Ooooo!" All the kids in Mrs. Rhodes' kindergarten class remarked when Lil' Stevie came in the door in his Easter suit. "WOW," many of them continued, adding in a few Ooooo's and Ahhhh's for flavor. Stevie sure felt special. Meanwhile, later that morning, Ms. Fitzhugh woke up with a scream!

"I can't believe what time it is! I've got to get Stevie to school!" she said. When she reached Lil' Stevie's bedroom and found it empty, it was her turn to panic. "Where IS that boy? I know he didn't walk all the way to school by himself."

Her heart was pounding. She quickly got dressed and walked to the school. Stevie was surprised to see his

The Adventures of Lil' Stevie

mother show up at the school. But not as surprised as she was to see Stevie in his Easter suit. At this point she was more amused than upset. "Stevie, you had me scared half to death. I didn't know where you were, honey."

"I couldn't wake you up, Mom, so I just let you sleep," Stevie explained.

That wasn't the last time his mom had an unusual effect on his school day. Something special about his mom was the way she decided how Stevie should dress for school. She did two things. She would always listen to the weather report on W.A.K.R. radio and then she'd open the front door and check outside to get a feel for the temperature for herself. One particular winter morning, Stevie's mother woke up cold. Before she even heard the weather forecast she was convinced this was going to be a cold one. She pulled out corduroy pants, which were very thick, an undershirt, a long-sleeved shirt, *and* a sweater for Stevie to wear. Then, much to Stevie's dismay, she pulled out the long johns. Long johns were long underwear that were very warm, made of cotton, and fit closely to your legs. These were usually reserved for those bitter cold days that you wanted to play outside.

"Mom, do I have to wear long johns?" Stevie petitioned.

"Baby, it's cold out there! You don't wanna freeze to death, do you?" she asked.

"But Mom, it's really not that cold out there. I'm gonna be burning up in class with those things on," Stevie replied.

"Stevie put those things on and get dressed for school before you end up late. I'm not gonna go back and forth with you over this. As cold as I am this morning, I know it's freezing out there."

Stevie put on his long johns. They were a tight fit... warm and tight. He then pulled his corduroy pants over his long johns. He put on his socks and shoes, but with all those clothes on he could barely stand up. His mother pulled out his heavy winter coat, hat, and scarf. He found his gloves in the pockets of his coat. Before he even left the house, Lil' Stevie was sweating pretty good. He thought for sure his mom was going to see his sweat and how difficult of a time he was having moving and just say "come back here and take those long johns off." But it didn't happen. Stevie was off to school with tight long johns hugging his legs for the whole day.

By the time Lil' Stevie got to school, his back was damp with sweat. He tore off his coat, hat, and scarf as soon as he was indoors. He noticed that none of the other students were wearing heavy winter coats. It seemed like most of the time that old boiler in the boiler room could never quite heat that school building. But today the classroom was about as warm as it could be. Just as Stevie expected, the sun came out and the outside temperature started to rise. The shades on the long windows in the classroom were all the way up, which permitted the sun to aim its bright warm rays into the classroom. Half of the classroom never got sun. Of course Stevie's desk was right in the middle of the half that did. This had to be the most uncomfortable day in Stevie's entire life. He was so hot, he couldn't think or concentrate. As soon as he settled in his mind that this was just going to be a hot day, it started.

He remembered how dry his legs were when he put on his long johns that morning. That long bath he had the night before dried up his skin thoroughly. Instead of putting lotion on his legs like his mom instructed, Lil' Stevie went straight to bed. Today he was paying the price. Just one tiny little itch on the back of his leg was all it took to begin the nightmare. Stevie reached down and scratched with exactly four scrapes of his fingernails on the back of his leg. As his little fingers dug into his leg through the corduroy and cotton long johns it brought momentary, soothing relief.

Then, almost as if someone had a voodoo doll of him and were causing the itching through a dark magic, Stevie's other leg began in the same spot.

Scratch! Scratch! Scratch! Scratch!

Stevie again found relief in scratching. Next it was his thigh that itched.

Scratch! Scratch! Scratch! Scratch!

Then it was his opposite leg shin that itched.

Scratch! Scratch! Scratch! Scratch!

Then his hip, then his shin, then his leg again, then his hip again!

Scratch! Scratch! Scratch! Scratch! Scratch! Scratch! Scratch! Scratch!

Before Stevie knew it, he was scratching all over. It seemed like everywhere the long johns touched his body it felt like his skin was crawling. It was all-out war on his dry legs encased by long johns. Lil' Stevie couldn't find relief no matter how hard he scratched. It was difficult to reach the itching because of the thickness of the corduroys. So he scratched and rubbed and scratched and rubbed until he almost broke the skin on his legs. He couldn't be still. The other students were starting to laugh.

"Stephen, are you OK?" the teacher asked. By this time Lil' Stevie's itchy leg syndrome forced tears of frustration to puddle in his eyes. When the teacher called his name, it temporarily broke the itchy spell. Stevie went to his teacher's desk at the front and told his teacher his problem.

"My legs won't stop itching. They are so dry and my mom made me wear long johns today," he explained.

"Why did your mom make you wear long johns?" she asked.

"She was cold this morning and she usually helps me get dressed according to how she feels. She was really cold this morning," Stevie said.

The teacher opened her lower right desk drawer and pulled out a pink tube of something.

"Here Stephen, take my lotion with you to the lavatory and put some on your legs. That might help," she offered.

Stevie grabbed the lotion, thinking he'd try anything at this point. He quickly shoved the lotion in his front pocket. He was afraid someone might see him going into the bathroom with a tube of women's lotion. Weird! Butter on your face as lotion, that's one thing, but lady's pink lotion is a whole other something. Stevie entered the boy's bathroom

The Adventures of Lil' Stevie

and was glad to see no one else there. He quickly closed himself in the first stall. He pulled the lotion out of his pants pocket and placed it carefully on the toilet paper dispenser. As if his legs were on fire, he quickly unbuckled his belt and pulled down his corduroys. He pulled down his long johns as far as they would go. He then squirted the lotion into the palm of one hand and set the lotion back down. He rubbed the lotion between his hands and applied it to his legs. It really didn't make any noise, but in Stevie's head he was sure he heard, "Ssssssss," the hissing sound that's made when water is thrown on a campfire.

"AHHHHHH!" Stevie said out loud. "Wooo-Weee! That feels great!" Stevie used as much lotion as he could to moisturize his ashy legs. By the time he was done, he had his legs and the entire lavatory smelling just like his pretty teacher. He didn't mind. The agony was over. It didn't dawn on Stevie until later that he could have removed his long johns while in the bathroom. *But,* Stevie thought, *who wants to go back into the classroom or walk home carrying their winter underwear?* Stevie returned to the classroom with a huge smile on his face. Most students never see a classmate return from the restroom as pleased as Stevie was that day. They looked at him kind of funny.

Have you ever found yourself in a situation that seems like it has no answers? So many suffer when they don't have to. Just ask a trusted adult for help! The solution to Lil' Stevie's agony was in a drawer at the front of the class the entire time. As long as Stevie held on to his itchy secret and kept it to himself, the solution never came. But when he finally shared his situation with his teacher, his pain ended. You don't have to work it out by yourself. Whatever you are going through, there is a trusted adult somewhere around who has already been through the same thing and is willing to help you get through it, too. It was a warm walk home from school that day, but at least it wasn't itchy!

Bustin' Suds

"Beat the heat! Beat the heat!" Lil' Stevie's mom shouted to her kids as they lay sleeping on a summer Saturday morning. Even though it was summertime and school was out, it didn't mean the Fitzhugh kids could just lay in bed all morning. Ms. Fitzhugh had the responsibility of maintaining the household, but she was not going to do it all by herself, especially with four able-bodied kids in the house. "Get up now and beat the heat. If you stay in bed all morning you'll be sweating like a pig trying to get your work done while it's hot outside!" she warned.

It didn't matter much to Lil' Stevie. His mom never gave him hard chores. Sometimes he would vacuum, dust, or clean the windows. One thing he absolutely hated was cleaning the ashtrays. He'd have to gather the ashtrays from the living room, dining room, kitchen, and his mother's room. Next he would dump the ashes and cigarette butts in the trash. Then he would fill up the downstairs bathroom sink with soapy water and wash every single ashtray. Lil'

The Adventures of Lil' Stevie

Stevie hated the smell of smoke, the ashes, and the cigarette butts. His mom started smoking as a teen and continued to smoke cigarettes her entire life. Stevie tried to get her to stop, but she never did.

Chores were very important. The grass had to be cut, the clothes had to be washed, the kitchen had to be cleaned, the dishes had to be washed, the beds had to be made, and the list went on and on. Everybody had to help. Raymond usually cut the grass. At first, the Fitzhughs didn't have a lawn mower. Raymond would borrow Grandma's push mower. Sometimes Stevie's mom would pay Jeff, the teenage boy next door, to cut the grass because they had a real lawnmower. Chucky was good with the laundry and making sure the house was just plain neat and clean. There were times, before they had a washer and dryer or when they were broken, the laundry had to be taken to the Laundromat on Copley Road. Stevie would jump at the chance to go to the Laundromat. Raymond and Chucky would load the clothes into the car. They'd take up most of the back seat. This was one of the only times Lil' Stevie got to ride in the front seat. At the Laundromat, Stevie and his mom would roll one of the carts out to the car. They would load it up with clothes and push it back inside.

"These clothes are heavy, Mom!" Lil' Stevie remarked.

"We don't have to take them all at once," his mom replied.

"I can do it, Mom!" Lil' Stevie boasted. His mom watched him struggle to get the cart full of clothes through the door. The only thing Stevie didn't like about the

Laundromat was sometimes there were some pretty weird people that drifted in and out. Although it was mostly empty today, this happened to be one of those crazy times.

"Stevie, go check and see if there are 3 washers open down there and a Bigboy while I sort these clothes." A Bigboy was a heavy-duty washer Stevie's mom used to wash blankets and other big things.

"Mom, there's a strange man down there looking at me," Stevie said with a little shakiness in his voice. He didn't want to actually admit that he was scared.

"That man ain't thinking about you, boy, go save my washers for me," she replied. Stevie walked down to the row of washers, keeping an eye on the man in the corner the whole time. The closer he got to the washer the more he heard the man talking to himself.

"They told me the sun wasn't a star... the sun is a star... it is the closest star... I know the sun is a star... don't talk to me like that... I talk the way I want to talk, this is my mouth!" the man mumbled these things to himself out loud.

Who is this man talking to? Stevie thought to himself, looking around to confirm there was no one else there. *This is way too scary for me.*

He saved the washers and the Bigboy and ran back to his mother. "Mom, that man was talking to his self," Stevie said with a giggle. He was quickly confronted by his mom.

"I hope you are not laughing at him! That's not nice. Sometimes people have issues they can't work out and they end up trying to work them out in their mind and they never stop. You don't know what he's been through," his mom

The Adventures of Lil' Stevie

explained. Mom always impressed Stevie. She was always thoughtful, always kind, always hardworking. They finished the clothes and made their way back home.

The dishes were a different issue. The Fitzhughs had a dishwasher, but it never worked. Instead Greta usually did the dishes and at times Raymond or Chucky would alternate to help. They washed the dishes in the sink and used the dishwasher as a dish rack. One weeknight after dinner, Greta had to rush upstairs to finish her homework. For her sweet sixteen birthday, Mom surprised her with her own desk. It wasn't a store-bought desk, but one Mom made out of two crates. It had a piece of plywood for a top and it had a huge mirror. Greta loved that desk. Lil' Stevie called it a desk, his mom called it a vanity. Lil' Stevie liked the word "desk" better; he didn't know what a "vanity" was. That's where Greta did her homework.

"Chucky go in there and do those dishes, your sister has got a project to finish for school."

"Mom, how come Stevie never has to do the dishes?" Chucky asked.

"Stevie! Chucky's right. You need to start taking a turn to do these dishes," their mother announced.

"Mom," Stevie started sadly, "I'm sorry but I just won't be able to do the dishes tonight. I've got waaaaaay too much homework to do," Stevie explained.

"It's not going to take you but a few minutes to wipe up these few dishes. Go ahead and get started and you'll have plenty of time to do your homework," Ms. Fitzhugh said. Lil' Stevie was determined that he was not ready to start participating in the dish-washer rotation, bustin' suds. He moaned and groaned and sulked and complained, but it didn't work. His mom was insistent. Tonight would be his first night to wash dishes.

"Awe Mom... I can't stand up that long. It's gonna hurt my back," Stevie argued. His argument fell on deaf ears. His mom didn't budge. "I'm not tall enough to reach all the way into the sink." His mom just shook her head in disbelief of all of Stevie's foolish excuses. Then Lil' Stevie had a thought. If it takes me a long time to wash the dishes, I won't have time to do my homework. Mom won't let ANYTHING interfere with homework.

Stevie began to prepare for his marathon dishwashing session. He grabbed a stool and placed it in front of the sink. He climbed up on the stool, filled one of the two sink basins with warm, soapy water. He used the other basin to rinse the dishes. That's the way he saw Chucky do it. He put all of the dirty dishes in the soapy water and grabbed the dishtowel to begin to wash. He washed each dish as slowly as he possibly could. If it were a movie, you would think he was moving in slow-motion. He slowly picked up a dish out of the soapy water then s-l-o-w-l-y wiped it with the dishcloth. Then, as slowly as he could, he would turn the faucet on to let the water rinse a dish for several minutes. Finally he'd load the clean dish in the rack inside the broken dishwasher to dry. It took Stevie TWO HOURS to finish the dishes.

When he finished, he hopped down from the stool (that he really didn't need) and approached his mother who was sitting in the living room.

The Adventures of Lil' Stevie

"Mom, I'm all finished with the dishes," he reported. "It looks like it's already bedtime." He gave a big, exaggerated yawn and a stretch. "I won't be able to get to my homework because the dishes took so long to do."

"Well Stevie, you are right. It did take a long time. But since you are such a good worker, I'm gonna let you stay up late to finsh your homework," she said.

This was not going according to plan, Stevie thought. He was really ready to go to bed, not stay up late to do homework. His mom got up and went into the kitchen. Stevie grabbed the worksheets assigned for homework. As soon as he sat down to do his homework, he heard a horrifying sound, DISHES! He jumped up and ran into the kitchen.

"NOOO!" Stevie screamed. He saw his mom taking all the dishes out of the broken dishwasher and loading them back into the sink with fresh warm soapy water. "What are you doing, Mom?" Stevie asked feverishly.

"I inspected your dishwashing job and I found too many poorly washed. The best thing for you to do is to wash them ALL over. It's how you do what you are supposed to do when no one else is around that tells everybody what kind of person you really are," his mom instructed. Stevie stood at the sink and washed all the dishes the way they were supposed to have been washed. In addition he had to stay up late to finish his homework. Boy, was he sleepy!

Lil' Stevie was "bustin' suds" all night. Your character is built when you do something with excellence that you really don't want to do. Strong character is what it takes to be a champion in life. If there is anything that you are assigned to do, do it as best as it can be done, whether someone is watching or not. If you have to spend your valuable time doing it, then it's worth doing well. If not, you may end up doing what could been done once all over again just to get it right.

Breaking the Rules

There were times Lil' Stevie found himself home alone. He never thought about whether it was right, wrong, or dangerous. It's just the way it was. His mom would tell him to play in his room until she got back. Lil' Stevie didn't mind because he could turn any day locked inside the house into an adventure. Sometimes he could not play outside because of the rain. He would have to find something exciting to do inside. Once, at Grandma's house, all the kids were stuck inside because of the rain.

"Why is it raining so hard, Grandma?" Stevie asked his grandmother.

"Muhva naycha s'gotta scrub her flo' b'fo she lay down her green cawpet," Grandma said.

"I never thought about it like that!" Lil' Stevie responded.

One of his favorite adventures was to play sheriff. He would put on his cowboy gun belt that he got for Christmas with his cap gun in the holster. Although he and Chucky slept in bunk beds, they would often unbunk the beds to

The Adventures of Lil' Stevie

make their room different. With the bunk beds down Stevie would put his pillow over the short footboard at the foot of the bed. It was about as high as Stevie's waist when he stood there. That was his horse, and the pillow was his saddle. He secured the saddle by wrapping his belt around the pillow and footboard. He would tie another belt around the bedpost to be used as reigns. Sheriff Fitzhugh of the Wild, Wild West would climb up on his horse and hunt the Most Wanted criminals to get the reward.

Sometimes he would pretend he was a special agent assigned to protect the house. He had an air rifle that didn't shoot anything. Lil' Stevie stood at the front window of his bedroom. Imaginary attackers pulled up in front of the house, jumped out of their vehicles, and attempted to overtake the complex. Agent Lil' Stevie defeated them all! They turned back because Agent Lil' Stevie was too clever, too quick... too good.

Just like there were many ways he beat boredom, there were also many ways he solved his problems. Probably the biggest problem Stevie wished he could solve was with his mom and dad. They were not together. Some of his friends had the same situation. Stevie didn't have an explanation or solution. It was just something he had to deal with. He tried not to think about it. But when he did, it made him sad. So he found a way to cope. Sometimes when Stevie felt really sad, he would walk down the street to the corner of Slosson Street and Roslyn Avenue. He would go up Slosson Street towards Schumacher School. Halfway up the block was a perfect tree to climb. Lil' Stevie would climb that tree. High in the tree there was a perfect spot to sit. The branches at that spot almost made what looked like a chair. Stevie fit perfectly in that chair. When Stevie was sad, sitting in the "Tree Chair" made him feel invisible. People would walk up and down Slosson Street. No one ever saw Lil' Stevie nestled high in the tree. He was invisible. Somehow his problems at that moment disappeared, too. Especially in the fall when the leaves burst into a fiery orange and yellow color. On days like that, no matter what direction Stevie looked while he was in the tree, there was beauty all around. Sometimes Stevie would be in the tree for a very long time. When he came down, he was reminded that no matter how ugly life became, if you look hard enough, you'll find beauty around you.

One of Lil' Stevie's favorite activities was to ride his bike. Chucky was the bike riding king. Chucky could ride with no hands *and* pop a wheelie! What was even more awesome was that Chucky could *ride* a wheelie! A lot of kids could pop a wheelie. That's when you jerk the front end of the bike up off the ground and you are only on your back wheel then you go back down. Riding a wheelie is when you pop a wheelie and keep riding while only on your back wheel. Bike riding came with certain rules. Stevie could only ride on the sidewalk. Chucky was experienced enough to ride in the street. Stevie could only cross at the corners, with permission, and there was no crossing between two parked cars. He had to look both ways before crossing. After a while, racing up and down the sidewalk got really boring. All the other kids were riding in the street, crossing the

The Adventures of Lil' Stevie

street, and turning the corner.

My mom is just being mean to me, Stevie thought as he passed his house again. His mom was sitting on the front porch talking with Mrs. Tate, the next-door neighbor. On his next pass he noticed a car in the driveway. It was his Aunt Sarah. She and Stevie's mom went in the house. Stevie was officially "unsupervised!"

My next time down the street I'm gonna cross the street. Mom won't even care, Lil' Stevie plotted. He raced down to the corner. He looked both ways for cars before bolting across the street into new territory. He raced partly up the hill before turning around and zooming back to the corner and coming back to his side of the street. He raced his bike back past his house in the other direction.

"Great! Mom is still inside with Aunt Sarah!" he said out loud to himself. He popped a baby wheelie and zoomed to the other corner. He stopped, looked both ways, and pedaled fast across the street into even more new territory. His heart raced. He was so excited, he wanted to tell his mom he crossed the street safely. He knew he'd get a spanking, though, for doing it without permission. He turned around and safely returned to his rightful side of the street. He was now ready to repeat the entire route with confidence. As he whizzed past his home, he saw his friends: the Stark sisters, Rusty, and Flower. They were on the other side of the street. Instead of going all the way to the corner, Stevie decided to cross the street at the Tate's driveway. Without looking, he darted out of the driveway and into the street. Immediately he heard the screeching of tires. It was too late for the car to stop and too fast for Stevie to change directions. The car careened into the back wheel of Lil' Stevie's bike. The impact flattened the bike and launched Stevie ten feet into the air. The driver never saw Stevie because Stevie dashed out from between two parked cars. Everybody on the ten hundred block of Roslyn Avenue came out of their homes and gathered around to see who was involved in the accident.

"STEVIE GOT HIT BY A CAR! Go get Ms. Fitzhugh!" someone screamed. One of the most fearful accidents one could ever experience is to get hit by a car! Stevie lay motionless in the street for a moment before bursting into tears. Stevie got away with just a few scratches. Stevie cried more because he knew he'd been "hit by a car" than from the actual result of being hit by a car. His mother and Aunt Sarah bolted out of the house to investigate the drama outside. Ms. Fitzhugh heard someone say Stevie's name. His mother's panic subsided when she saw that he would be OK.

"What were you doing in the street, son?" she asked.

Stevie pretended like he could not speak through his tears. He knew he was not supposed to be in the street with his bike. He hoped his mom would feel sorry for him. Maybe he wouldn't get in trouble.

"Is he OK?" the driver of the car asked. She was more terrified than Stevie. She was a young driver who had never been in an accident before. She wasn't speeding or distracted. "I didn't see him. I'm so sorry," she said, fighting back her own tears.

The Adventures of Lil' Stevie

"Don't worry about it, baby," Stevie's mom told the young driver. "I've told that boy a thousand times to only cross at the corner and NEVER cross between two parked cars! Besides ain't nothing wrong with him, other than a few scratches and hurt feelings."

There was no need to call for the ambulance or police. Stevie and the driver were both a little shaken up, but there were no serious injuries or damage. Later that night, Stevie got a good talking to from his mom, but managed to avoid punishment for breaking the rules. Getting hit by the car was punishment enough. Stevie knew how wrong he was to disobey.

"Mom," Stevie interrupted, "I'm sorry for what I did."

"I know you are," Stevie's mother said with a smile. She tried to keep Stevie from getting too down on himself. She knew Stevie learned a powerful lesson that day. "I accept your apology son, I hope you will do better next time." She gave Lil' Stevie a big hug. "As soon as I get a little extra money, we'll see about getting that bike fixed, if you can stay out of the street!"

That day, Stevie learned that rules are there for a reason. His mom wasn't being mean by insisting he stay out of the street or by making him only cross at the corner. She was protecting him. Stop signs were at the corners. It's safe to cross there because drivers must stop. Children can't be seen when they cross between parked cars. It's the most dangerous there. When you break the rules, you lose your protection. You put yourself at risk. It's the same way in life.

When you break the rules in life, the lessons learned could be very painful. Stevie was very fortunate he wasn't seriously hurt. It doesn't always turn out that way. After this experience, he became more determined to obey the rules, whether his mom was around or not. He did not want to lose his protection.

The Roslyn Sledding Championship

The Fitzhugh's backyard hill was perfect for sledding. It wasn't too steep, it wasn't too flat, and it wasn't too short. It was just right. And because it was just right, kids up and down Roslyn Avenue stopped by the Fitzhugh's house any Saturday after a big snow to see if Raymond, Chucky, and Stevie were sledding on their hill. If they were, it would be pure sledding fun for hours until your feet and hands were too cold to stay outside any longer.

Raymond was the fastest because no one could get a running start like he did. He would pick up that old "Flexible Flyer Sled" (the sled that steers), run 4 or 5 strong strides, and dive onto that sled chest-first with lightning speed.

ZOOM!

He would zip past onlookers standing on either side of the hill. There were two directions you could take the hill. The first was straight on. It was the steeper of the two routes. They called that the "Cherry Tree" slope because it

The Adventures of Lil' Stevie

was closest to the cherry tree. As the hill flattened out, you would end up going over a small jump at the end caused by an old wooden railroad tie at the border of the Fitzhugh property. The other slope (which didn't have a name, it was just the other slope) was longer, but slower. It went along the other side of the cherry tree on one side with the patio on the other. It forced you to start left, but curve your ride back to the center of the backyard toward the bushes along the back border of the Fitzhugh yard. You had to be very careful. There was only one break in the bushes for you pass through if you had enough speed. It was over into the neighbor's yard right behind the Fitzhugh's. If you couldn't steer well, you'd crash into the bushes. It happened quite a bit with people who took this slope.

"Wow!" Stevie said as Raymond zipped by once again. "How does he do that?"

"He's just that fast, Stevie!" Chucky answered. Chucky was no slouch, either. He was more adventurous. He could go down on his chest, sitting up, or even standing up. Once Chucky even slid down the hill without a sled. He was skiing without skis. Lil' Stevie wasn't good enough or strong enough to use the big kids' sled. The Flexible Flyer was made with a wooden top and had a wooden steering piece that looked more like a boomerang attached to the front of the sled. The metal ski parts were red. You could either lie on your stomach and steer with your hands or sit upright and steer with your feet. Stevie usually went down the hill in a plastic, disc-like saucer. He spun around more than he slid. It wasn't very fast, but his mom thought he was safer in it than he'd be in the Flyer. Stevie had to get his fun in quick because it seemed like he got cold faster than anyone else. One time, his toes froze! By the time he got inside to warm up he couldn't feel them, they were numb from the cold.

"Mom, I can't feel my toes!" he cried to his mother. "What do I do?"

"First, we've got to get you out of those wet clothes and into something dry and warm," she said. Stevie didn't even realize that his socks were damp. He quickly changed into the dry clothing his mom laid out for him. Slowly the feeling started to come back to his feet, and BOY DID IT HURT!

"Ow, Ow, Ow, Ow, Ow!" he cried.

As his feet and toes began to thaw, a pain he had never experienced began to throb in his feet. Stevie didn't know anything about frostbite nor had he ever heard of it. Frostbite is when the skin actually begins to die because it has gotten too cold. The pain Stevie was experiencing was the result of frostbite starting in his frozen feet and hands. Stevie spent the next half hour sitting near the heater vent in the living room. He was really hot. Soon he felt back to normal. Later Raymond and Chucky came in from outdoors to begin their thawing process. It was not as severe as Lil' Stevie's because they were better prepared for the cold and snow.

"Who wants hot chocolate?" his mom asked, knowing all hands would go up.

"I do!" Stevie shouted first.

"You know I do, too," Raymond confessed.

"Me too," Chucky said. As their mom fixed hot chocolate, the boys overheard a familiar announcement on the radio.

"The national weather service advisory has issued a winter storm warning in effect until 6 AM in the following counties… Portage… Stark… Cuyahoga… Summit…" the reporter said on the radio. That's all the boys needed to hear, SUMMIT COUNTY! Snow was coming to Akron. All kids want snow to hit on Sunday night! It may mean a three-day weekend if school is called off on Monday. The boys finished their hot drinks and began getting excited about the pending snowfall.

"Chucky, if there's no school tomorrow we can sled all day, come inside, get warm, and sled some more!" Stevie said with excitement.

"Stevie, if there is no school tomorrow, I'm gonna sleep until 12 noon, then sled all day," Chucky responded. Raymond jumped in.

"If there is no school tomorrow, I'm gonna sleep 'til noon, eat 'til one, then sled all day."

The boys stayed up to watch the 11 o'clock news. Some schools had already announced to be closed on Monday. It was not uncommon for all the schools to close except for the Akron schools. Stevie was never really interested in watching the news. Most of the time he was already in bed. If he were up and the news came on, he would turn the channel. Not tonight. The boys were listening to school closures for Monday. They had missed the segment where they announced the closings, now they were just reading the updated list scrolling across the bottom of the screen in alphabetical order. There it was, they all saw it at the same time: AKRON PUBLIC SCHOOLS!

"WOOO-WHOOO!" Stevie shouted. Raymond was relieved because he didn't quite finish his homework. It was official... no school tomorrow.

"Raymond, before you go to bed I want you to plug in the pipe warmer under the house," their mom instructed. "It's going to get cold tonight."

Sometimes when the temperature dropped really low, the water pipe would freeze. Stevie's mom bought something that wrapped around the pipe to keep it warm enough not to freeze. Frozen water pipes can burst. That's a big mess. It happened only one time at the Fitzhugh house. Ms. Fitzhugh was determined that it not happen again. Raymond and Chucky both went under the house through the tiny crawl space to plug in the warmer. Chucky held the flashlight while Raymond did the crawling. Stevie did the watching from the kitchen window.

When they finished they didn't come back in right away. As Stevie watched from the kitchen window, he saw something quite strange; something he had not seen before. Raymond and Chucky, with snow falling thick and heavy, began to sweep the slopes with a broom.

That's silly, Stevie thought. *Why are my brothers sweeping snow off of the sledding slopes?*

When the boys came in, that's the first thing Stevie asked. "Why did you guys do that?"

"What?" Chucky responded.

"That sweeping," said Stevie.

"You'll see," Raymond said. Chucky and Raymond got the biggest pots in the cupboard and filled them with water. They took the pots of water outside and poured them on the sledding slopes. After several trips, they swept the snow on top of the wet slopes and came back inside.

"You guys are soooo smart! That's going to make sledding tomorrow super-fast!" Stevie said. It snowed all night. The water froze on the hill. Under that freshly fallen snow was all ICE! The next day, Chucky helped Stevie prepare to stay warm while sledding.

"Stevie you got to put layers on, man, if you gonna stay warm," Chucky instructed. "You need to put your long john shirt and long john bottoms on first. Then put on a pair of thick pants and a pair of jeans on top of that. Before you put on your jeans, make sure you tuck your thick pants into your socks at the bottom. Put on another pair of thick socks on top of your first pair."

Chucky knew all the tricks to keep snow off of your skin. He showed Stevie how to put a small hole at the wrist of both of the sleeves of his long john shirt. Then you stretch the sleeve down over your hand and poke your thumb through the holes to keep it there. That way when you put your gloves and coat on, your wrists stay covered and no snow gets on your skin or down to your hand or arm. Stevie was more than ready this time. Before he even got outside to join Chucky and Raymond, kids from the neighborhood had already arrived. Some had brought their own sled, others rotated with the Fitzhugh's sled.

"Boy is this hill fast!" Stevie said in amazement. It was so icy you had to find fresh snow on the sides to even get back up the hill. Cherry Tree Slope was super-slick! Almost everyone taking that slope ended up "getting air" over the railroad tie and going farther than ever before into the neighbor's backyard. On the other slope, kids were plowing uncontrollably into the bushes in the backyard because they were going too fast to steer their sleds through the tunnel opening of the bushes.

"This is so much fun!" Stevie shouted to Chucky.

Just then Raymond ran by with the Flexible Flyer at his side. WHOOSH! Everyone stood back to see the fastest guy leap into air and land chest-first on the sled, barreling down Cherry Tree Slope. Quicker than anyone else had done, Raymond ramped over the snow-packed railroad tie and the end of the backyard. He soared at least three feet into the air and didn't land for what seemed like forever. Everyone strained to see just how far he would go! Raymond went ALL THE WAY TO THE NEIGHBOR'S DRIVEWAY! That's almost the entire width of the block. Everyone applauded and cheered Raymond as he returned. Stevie was proud to be Raymond's little brother.

"Stevie," Chucky called, "why don't you try the Flyer?"

"No, Mom said just to use the saucer. You tryin' to get me in trouble, man?" It made Stevie feel cool when he called somebody "man" like Chucky did. He didn't know how that got started, he just talked liked that with Chucky

The Adventures of Lil' Stevie

sometimes.

"Stevie! Man, you are NOT going to get in trouble. Just try it once and see how you like it. Don't lie down, sit up and steer with your feet. To turn right press with your left foot, to turn left press with your right. You're not scared are you, man?" Nobody wants to be labeled a 'fraidy-cat, afraid of accepting a challenge. Stevie thought about it.

"I'm not scared!"

"Then let's go," Chucky said.

"OK, let's go!" Stevie said, acting bravely. It was his first time on the Flexible Flyer. He was scared to death. He just couldn't show it. He didn't run into his take-off on the hill for extra speed like Raymond did. He set the sled at the top of the slow slope. He put his feet on the steering piece that looked like a boomerang. It had a rope attached to it for riders who were sitting upright to hold onto. Lil' Stevie's heart was beating like a bass drum. Before he took off, he looked around to see if anyone heard the pounding of his heart. He was sweating gobs of sweat, partly because he had on a million layers of clothes, but also because he was about to go down on the Flyer for the first time. It was no big deal to anybody else, but to Stevie it was like climbing Mount Everest! He was ready.

Scoot. Scoot. Scoot.

Stevie slowly inched towards the crest of the slow slope. All of the sudden, he felt two hands across the top of his back push him quickly down the hill. He heard Chucky laughing in his ear as he shoved Lil' Stevie as hard as he could. Chucky had to have pushed Stevie halfway down the hill, laughing and slipping on the ice himself.

"Chucky NOOOOOOOO!" Stevie screamed as he took off flying down the hill as if he had wings. "HEEEEELLLLLPPPPP!"

Stevie was headed straight toward the bushes. The laughter and voices of everyone at the top of the hill grew faint. All Lil' Stevie could hear was the metal skis of the Flexible Flyer cutting through the snow and ice at a lightning pace. Directly in front of Stevie was the thick bush so many of the other kids had crashed into all day. Closer. Closer. Closer. Stevie's eyes grew bigger and bigger. He held on tightly to the rope. *To turn right press with your left foot...* Stevie remembered Chucky's instructions. At the last second Stevie did what so many of the other boys, even the big kids, couldn't do that day. He pressed hard at the right time with his left foot and the sled made a perfect right turn into the tunnel through the bushes. The kids back at the top were amazed!

"STEVIE IS STILL GOING! HE MADE IT THROUGH THE BUSHES!" Chucky said in awe of his little brother. There was another problem. Not only was he still going, Stevie couldn't STOP!

"CHUCKYYYYYYYYY!" Lil' Stevie yelled. He was through the bushes and well into the neighbor's backyard approaching fast the longest mark made by Raymond. "HEEEEEEELPPP! I CAN'T STOP!"

No one had ever actually made it into the neighbor's driveway on Orlando Avenue, the street right behind Roslyn Avenue, where the Fitzhughs lived. Raymond made it *to* the driveway but not *into* it. No one knew that the driveway was icy and more slick than the backyard. And of course at the end of the drive was ORLANDO AVENUE... THE STREET! Stevie passed Raymond's mark. When the Flyer hit the driveway it picked up speed. Stevie was heading down the driveway directly to the street. He had no idea whether any cars were coming. If they were, he was certain they wouldn't be able to see him. He would be crushed. He had to do something. He had no brakes! There was nowhere to turn! He was almost at the sidewalk and next would come the street. At the last second, in what seemed like slow motion, Lil' Stevie released the rope and rolled off of the speeding sled. He felt like he was jumping out of a moving car. The sled sped through the street and popped over the curb at the other side. NO ONE had EVER gone that far before. Lucky for Stevie he didn't get hurt. Lucky for Chucky, too!

Stevie wasn't ready for the big kid's sled, not just yet. He became more concerned about what others would think if he "chickened out" than sticking to his convictions of what he was or was not ready for. Take your time. Don't rush growing up. In time all things change. There is a time for everything. It's important not to make decisions that you end up later wishing you had not made. The decisions that you make today are the seeds that grow your future. Think twice, then decide. A great future is grown by great decisions.

THE END

The ADVENTURES of LIL' STEVIE

BOOK 1: CANINES, CAMPOUTS, AND COUSINS

If you enjoyed this book, pick up a copy of the first book in the series. The Adventures of Lil' Stevie Book 1 is available through Amazon, Barnes & Noble, direct from Steve Fitzhugh, or order through your local book retailer. ISBN: 978-0-9919839-1-9

JOIN THE LIL' STEVIE WEBSITE: www.LilStevie.com or find Lil' Stevie on Facebook.

About the Author

Steve Fitzhugh is a nationally known and accomplished inspirational and motivational speaker. As a former member of the Denver Broncos of the National Football League, Steve has used his platform to reach over 1 million students in America with a message of hope, the value of good decision-making and the virtue of a committed drug-free lifestyle. Steve has successfully been able to blend his humor, experiences in the NFL, the story of his personal tragedy and his timeless antidotes of success and significance into engaging and entertaining presentations.

As an author, Steve articulately communicates through his writings with clear insights and easy to apply principles designed to help the reader become engaged in self-education and life-change. A husband, father, writer, poet, and life enthusiast, Steve has an uncommon ability to connect with both young and old with tools for personal success and professional effectiveness. Youth workers glean insights from his over 25 years of experience in work with students. Readers enjoy his writings and audiences enjoy his speaking, and the youth appreciate his ability to enter their world and spur them on to great heights and new precedents of accomplishment.

Connect with Steve: www.PowerMoves.org

Other books by Steve Fitzhugh:
Pastor, We Need A Bigger Boat
The Adventures of Lil' Stevie Book 1
How I Lost 50 Pounds in 5 Seconds

Who Will Survive?
Bringing the H.E.A.T.